Prehistoric Animals

PLATED DINOSAURS

WINDMILL
BOOKS ™

New York

Published in 2016 by **Windmill Books**,
an Imprint of Rosen Publishing
29 East 21st Street, New York, NY 10010

Designed and illustrated *by* David West

Cataloging-in-Publication Data
West, David.
Plated dinosaurs / by David West.
p. cm. — (Prehistoric animals)
Includes index.
ISBN 978-1-5081-9034-9 (pbk.)
ISBN 978-1-5081-9035-6 (6-pack)
ISBN 978-1-5081-9036-3 (library binding)
1. Ornithischia — Juvenile literature. 2. Dinosaurs — Juvenile literature.
I. West, David, 1956-. II. Title.
QE862.O65 W47 2016
567.915—d23

Manufactured in the United States of America
CPSIA Compliance Information: Batch #BW16PK: For Further Information contact Rosen Publishing, New York, New York at 1-800-237-9932

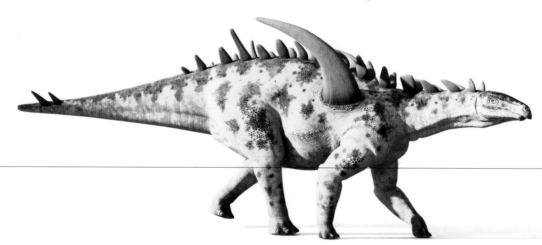

Contents

Crichtonsaurus means "Crichton's Lizard" after Michael Crichton, the author of Jurassic Park.

Although it had plates like a *Stegosaurus*, *Crichtonsaurus* was more closely related to *Ankylosaurus*.

Crichtonsaurus

CRY-ton-SAWR-us

This armored dinosaur had a strange collection of bony nodules along its back. Some stood upright to form small plates, like those of a *Stegosaurus*.

Crichtonsaurus grew up to 9.8 feet (3 m) in length and weighed 1 ton (0.9 metric ton).

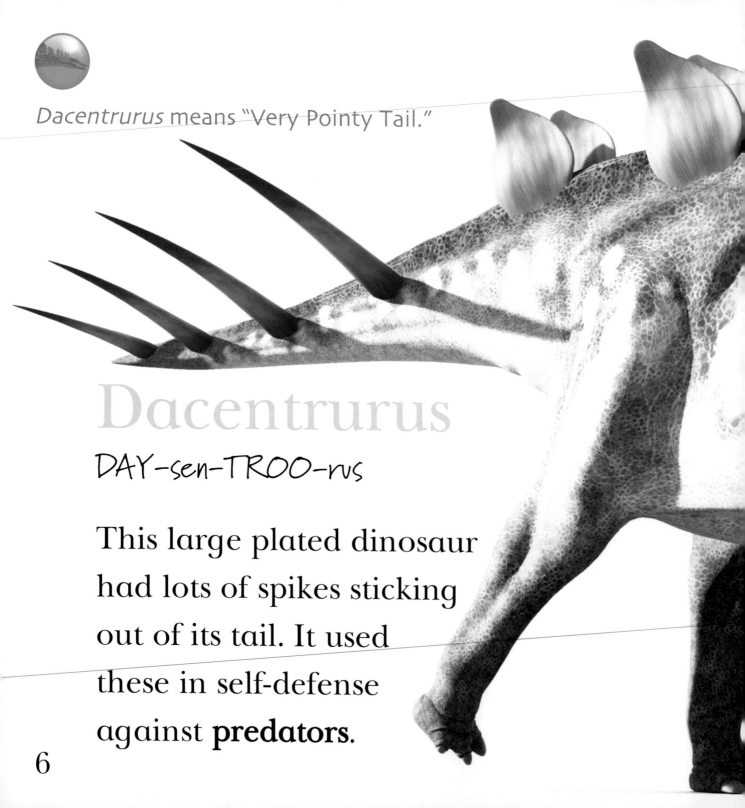

Dacentrurus means "Very Pointy Tail."

Dacentrurus

DAY-sen-TROO-rus

This large plated dinosaur had lots of spikes sticking out of its tail. It used these in self-defense against **predators**.

6

Dacentrurus grew to 19.7 feet (6 m) in length and weighed 2 tons (1.8 metric tons).

Fossils of this dinosaur have been found all over Europe. During the Upper Jurassic, much of Europe was a group of islands in a shallow sea.

Gigantspinosaurus

GIEE-gant-SPINE-oh-SAWR-us

This small plated dinosaur had a large, curved spike sticking out sideways from its shoulders.

The plates on the back of *Gigantspinosaurus* were small compared with other plated dinosaurs.

8

Gigantspinosaurus grew up to 14 feet (4.2 m) in length and weighed 1,500 pounds (680 kg).

Gigantspinosaurus means "Giant Spined Lizard."

Huayangosaurus

hwah-YAHNG-o-SAWR-us

Like many other plated
dinosaurs, *Huayangosaurus* had
a double row of plates down its back,
and spikes on its tail. Two large spikes
above its front legs helped to make it
look dangerous to a hungry predator.

10

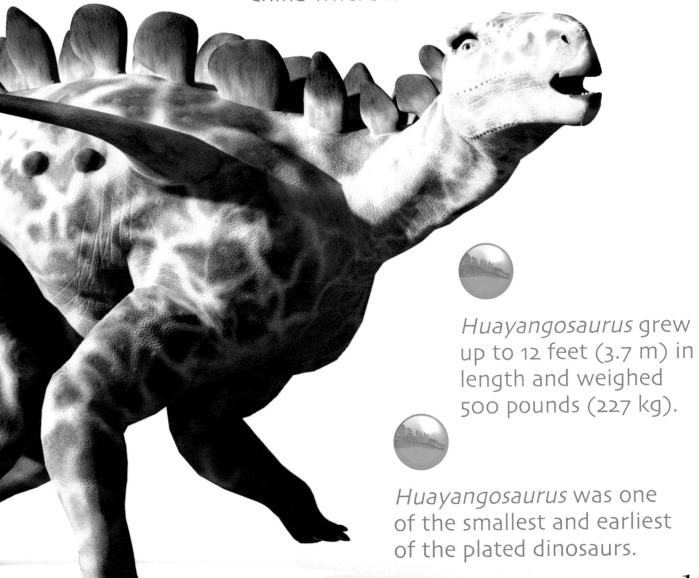

Huayangosaurus means "Huayang Lizard," named after the province in China where it was discovered.

Huayangosaurus grew up to 12 feet (3.7 m) in length and weighed 500 pounds (227 kg).

Huayangosaurus was one of the smallest and earliest of the plated dinosaurs.

11

Kentrosaurus

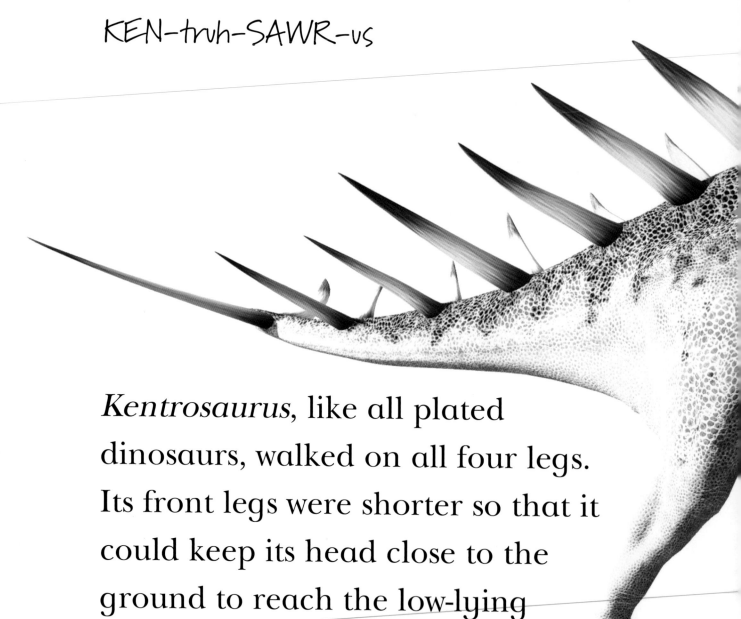

Kentrosaurus, like all plated dinosaurs, walked on all four legs. Its front legs were shorter so that it could keep its head close to the ground to reach the low-lying plants it fed on, such as **cycads**.

12

 *Kentrosaurus* means "Spiked Lizard."

Kentrosaurus grew up to 15 feet (4.5 m) in length and weighed 1.5 tons (1.4 metric tons).

Kentrosaurus had two rows of wicked spikes running down the length of its tail.

13

Lexovisaurus

lex–OH–vuh–SAWR–us

Similar to *Kentrosaurus*, this spiky, plated dinosaur had two rows of small plates and large spikes. It also had spikes protruding from its shoulders. Its tail ended in a set of spikes called a thagomizer.

The word "thagomizer" is taken from a dinosaur cartoon by Gary Larson.

Lexovisaurus grew up to 16.5 feet (5 m) in length and weighed around 2.2 tons (2 metric tons).

Lexovisaurus means "Lexovii Lizard," named after an ancient tribe from Europe.

15

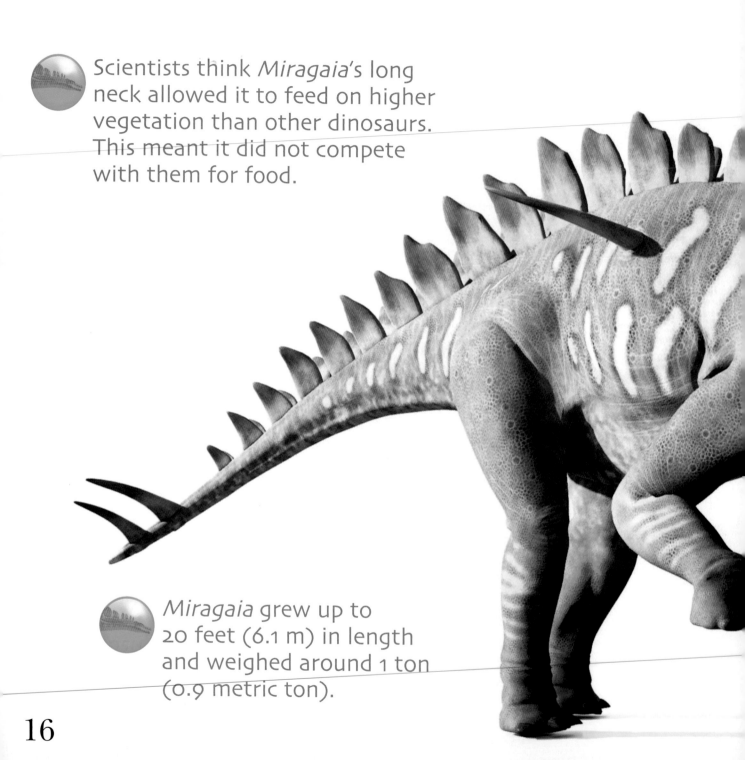

Scientists think *Miragaia*'s long neck allowed it to feed on higher vegetation than other dinosaurs. This meant it did not compete with them for food.

Miragaia grew up to 20 feet (6.1 m) in length and weighed around 1 ton (0.9 metric ton).

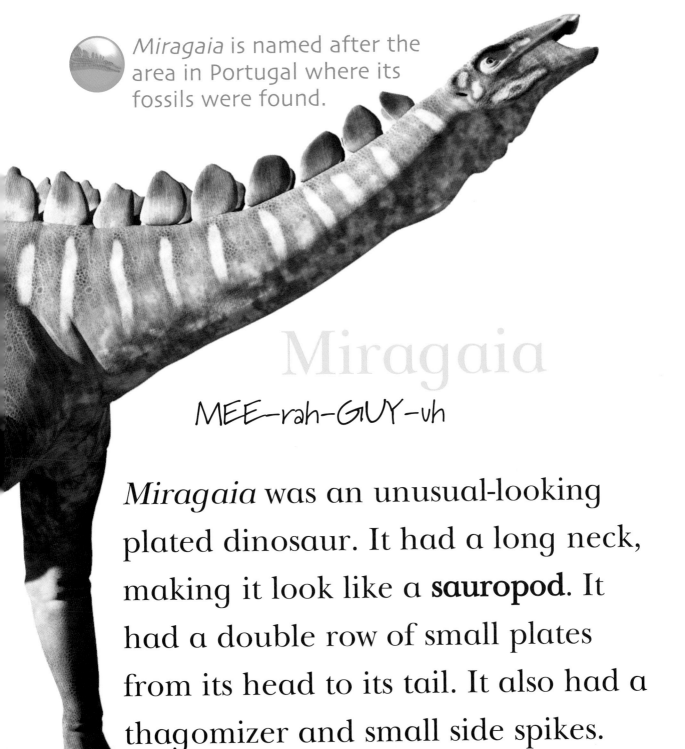

Miragaia is named after the area in Portugal where its fossils were found.

Miragaia

MEE—rah—GUY—uh

Miragaia was an unusual-looking plated dinosaur. It had a long neck, making it look like a **sauropod**. It had a double row of small plates from its head to its tail. It also had a thagomizer and small side spikes.

17

Stegosaurus

STEG-uh-SAWR-us

The large plates on *Stegosaurus*'s back may have contained blood vessels. Scientists think they could have helped control its body temperature, just like a car's radiator.

Stegosaurus means "Roof Lizard," after its large, bony plates.

When the fossils of *Stegosaurus* were first found, **paleontologists** thought that its plates lay flat on its back like roof tiles. This is how it got its name.

Stegosaurus grew up to 29.5 feet (9 m) in length and weighed 3.5 tons (3.1 metric tons).

19

Tuojiangosaurus

too-HWANG-o-SAWR-us

Tuojiangosaurus had a similar layout to most plated dinosaurs. The plates on its back, though, were thinner.

Like *Kentrosaurus*, it had a large spike sticking out sideways from each shoulder.

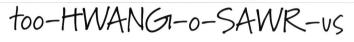

Tuojiangosaurus means "Tuo River Lizard."

Tuojiangosaurus was 23 feet (7 m) in length and 3 tons (2.7 metric tons) in weight.

The spines and plates that can be seen on plated dinosaurs were not attached to the skeleton. They grew out from the skin.

21

Wuerhosaurus means "Wuerho Lizard" from where its fossils were found in China.

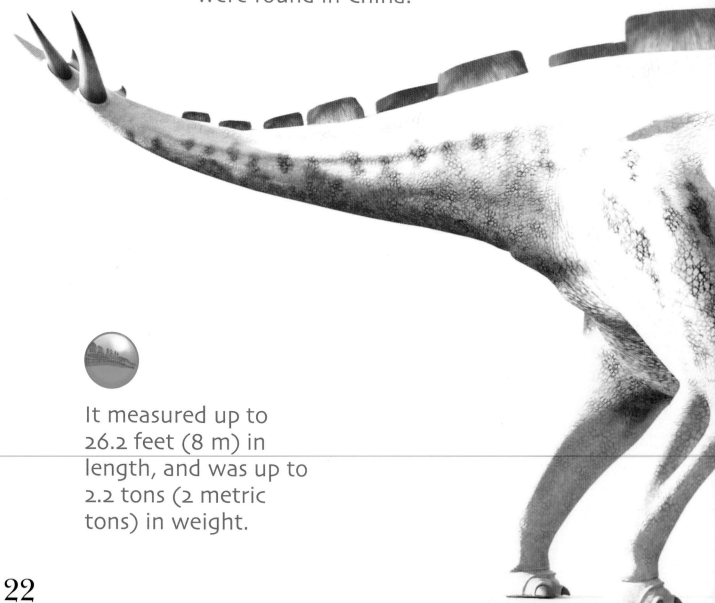

It measured up to 26.2 feet (8 m) in length, and was up to 2.2 tons (2 metric tons) in weight.

Wuerhosaurus

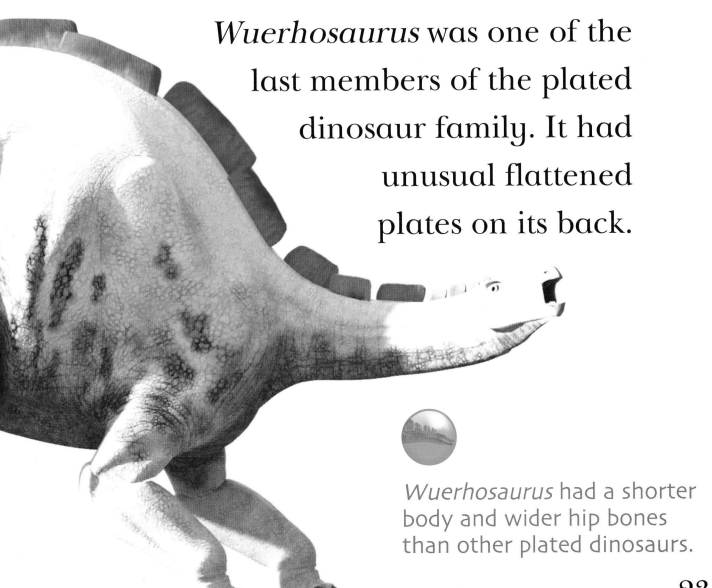

Wuerhosaurus was one of the last members of the plated dinosaur family. It had unusual flattened plates on its back.

Wuerhosaurus had a shorter body and wider hip bones than other plated dinosaurs.

23

Glossary

cycads
Palmlike plants.

paleontologists
Scientists who study early forms of life chiefly by examining fossils.

predators
Animals that hunt and kill other animals for food.

sauropod
A family of dinosaurs with long necks and long tails, such as *Diplodocus*.

Timeline

Dinosaurs lived during the Mesozoic Era, which is divided into three main periods.

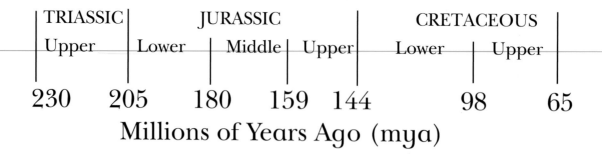

TRIASSIC		JURASSIC			CRETACEOUS	
Upper	Lower	Middle	Upper		Lower	Upper
230	205	180	159	144	98	65

Millions of Years Ago (mya)